The ABC's of Success in Simple Terms

The ABC's of Success in Simple Terms

Edward Paul Sowa

Illustrated by Callista Barrett

VANTAGE PRESS
New York

Published by Vantage Press, Inc.
419 Park Ave. South, New York, NY 10016

Manufactured in the United States of America
ISBN: 0-533-15039-6

Library of Congress Catalog Card No.: 2004096661

0 9 8 7 6 5 4 3 2 1

To the following people, who without their inspiration and guidance, this work would not have been possible:

My Family—Alfreda and Michael Sowa (my mother and father, both deceased), who brought me into this world and instilled in me proper values. My brother Michael, who gave me guidance when I needed it. My sister Annette, who gave care to the family when needed. My sister-in-law Helen, who gave advice when warranted.

My Business Family—The Wetteraus. The late Mr. Ted, Mark, and Conrad, who possess great values and believe in the word of God, and inspired me to the best that I can do.

My Friends—Larry Weiss and Bill Pocilujko, who always were there for me to offer advice on any subject, and Steve Venegas and Greg Lake, who have kept me young in their desire to achieve the pinnacle of success.

Contents

Discover

The ABC's of Success in Simple Terms

This book will give you insight into just what you can do with your life when you are inspired and focused. Mr. Successo will guide you through this simple journey. These simple premises have guided the author in his quest for success. Please sit back and enjoy the experience. It just may change your life!

"Mr. Successo"

I Believe in Myself

A

One Must Believe in One's Own Ability and Desire to Succeed!

There is no greater motivator than to be self-motivated. In life, we must believe in our own abilities—100 percent without reservation—to be a success! We must desire to succeed and put in the effort needed to achieve our desired results. One must set their own goals in life to strive for. Goals for some may be modest in nature—as making a decent living and raising their family to have the necessities of life. For others, the goal may be to be chairman of the board of AT&T and have all the wealth and prestige which go with the same. No matter what the self-goal is, you must believe in yourself that you have the ability, the resources, the intelligence to achieve your goal. If you do not believe you have these attributes, then your goal will not be achieved.

Moral: I believe in myself!

I Must Understand the System

B

One Must Believe in and Understand the System and Vehicle in Which One Wants to Be a Success!

If you do not believe life is fair and we all have the same opportunities to succeed—then failure will result. You must believe in the system! It may not be perfect but if you learn its idiosyncrasies and how to operate within it, your chance of success is very much enhanced. If one wants to be president, one knows it is possible within the realm of a democracy to do so, but it is a difficult task to do so in a country with a dictatorship. Hard work and astute political instincts can work to achieve your goal in a democratic nation. A revolution must be accomplished in a dictatorial state. A much harder task, indeed!

Moral: I must understand the system!

I Must Maintain My Health

C

One Must Be Health Conscious to Keep the Momentum Going!

If one does not care about one's physical condition, then that person may not be at the finish to reap the rewards of one's hard work. A yearly physical should be regularly scheduled in one's agenda to ensure physical health is maintained. Also, a regular regimen of exercise should be included in one's daily schedule. The program should be adhered to without deviation to keep the body in good shape. A body not properly maintained will be a road-block to success.

Moral: I must maintain my health!

D

One Must Be Extroverted to Climb the Ladder of Success!

Interaction with people is necessary for success. Introverts may be excellent computer operators, but extroverts will possess interactive skills that will aid them in their climb to the top. Extroverts who communicate well will accomplish tasks sooner than others who lack these attributes. Nobody is better than you are! Go out into the world and let them know it!

Moral: I will be an extrovert!

I Believe in a Higher Being

E

Religious Values Are a Positive Influence to Success!

We all must believe in a higher being whether it be God, Allah, or the infinite power from above. A person needs someone . . . something . . . to believe in. Believing gives us hope! Believing gives us a reason to go on in the face of obstacles. Believing helps us to achieve and helps us to reason. Our believing can be silent, but it must be in our mind. Believing is a personal value that should be respected by all.

Moral: I believe in a higher being!

I Will be Creative

F

Creativity Counts!

There are more ways than one to climb a mountain. There are also more ways than one to climb the mountain of success to the pinnacle. Creative people cause things to happen. Creativity spawns innovation! One must always look for alternative routes and ideas as we progress with our lives on the road to success. Take time in your life to stop and let the creative juices of the mind ferment and come forth with new ideas and innovations. The road to success will be easier to achieve!

Moral: I will be creative!

I Will Remain Focused

G

One Must Remain Focused to Succeed!

To achieve at any level one cannot fluctuate between goals and deviate from objectives. One must remain focused on your objective and direct all your efforts toward obtaining the goal. If a stockbroker's goal is to be the best investor in the stock market, the broker must study all facts pertaining to the stocks listed on the major exchanges and become an expert on such. The broker cannot change one's course midstream and decide to study the commodities market if one's goal is still the stock market. That is an entirely different entity and will be a negative influence on one's main objective.

Moral: I will remain focused!

I Will Win

H

Winning Is What Life Is All About!

All of us are competitive by nature. Add to this fact the strong desire to succeed and we all want to win. To do so, we must pass the competition on the road to the summit. It is not a sin to win. The better-conditioned athlete will win the race. The more intelligent businessman will win in the business world. We must set our sights high and must always remember our goal is to win—not second or third place but first. Strive to be the best!

Moral: I will win!

I Will Control Stress

I

Stress Must Be Addressed and Controlled to Be a Success!

In everyone's life comes periods of anxiety and extreme stress. This stress must be addressed or it will hinder or derail the journey toward success. We must stop, relax, and smell the roses as we proceed on our quest. We do not have to get to the pinnacle of success today. Our path should be ever upward at a reasonable pace. We will enjoy the ascent and be able to physically and mentally accomplish it in this manner.

Moral: I will control stress!

I Will Document the Route to the Top

J

How You Reach the Top Is Most Important, for You May Have to Retrace Your Steps!

As we proceed through life, there will always be setbacks. We must always be prepared for these setbacks by documenting our path to success. If we are driving to an unknown destination and find we are lost, we can always pull the map, regroup, and get back on the correct route. The road to success is similar, and we must always have our map documented to fall back on if needed.

Moral: I will document the route to the top!

I Don't Need "Big Words" to Achieve

K

You Don't Need to Know Big Words or Phrases to Succeed!

These days most business and motivational books written feel that a new language and big words must be developed for success to happen. This is not so. Words in vogue such as *paradigm* of ancient Greek origin and the more recent proactive approach to problem-solving may look good in print, but are not necessary for success. People have been successful long before catchy words and phrases have evolved—before they have been empowered.

Moral: I don't need big words to achieve!

I Believe People are Good

L

One Must Believe that Most People Are Good, Honest and Want to Pursue the Right Path in Life!

As we proceed on the path of life, we must believe that all people are basically honest and well-intentioned. If we do not believe this, we will go through life with a persecution complex and we will always be looking over our shoulders and watching our backs. This is counterproductive in the pursuit of success. Cautious optimism is permissible, but skepticism is a detriment.

Moral: I believe people are good!

I Will Have Friends

M

Interpersonal Relationships Are Important!

It is very important to have friends and acquaintances to use as a sounding board for various thoughts and ideas. It is also good for the soul to have a few confidants you can trust with your inner feelings, desires, and disappointments. We all need someone to talk to and to lean on in times of need. Isolationism breeds insecurities.

Moral: I will have friends!

I Need My Family

N

Family Must Be the Single Most Important Factor to One's Well-being!

Having family ties are very important to one's sense of belonging, and being a functional part of such a relationship is key to being successful. After a hard day at work, it soothes the mind to come home and be met by loving children who are glad you are there. They ask how you are and tell of their day's activities. They jump up on your lap and want to be close. The bond is there! Stability abounds.

Moral: I need my family!

O

There Is a Time to Think, and a Time Not to Think—Hobbies Are Important!

One cannot continuously think or be on—burn-out will occur. At times, one must rest their mind and relax, take part in a hobby, whatever that might be. Peace of mind is good for the soul. For some, it may be a walk in the park communicating with the beauty of nature. For others, it may be collecting toy trains or coins. Still others may relax by resting on a hammock in the great outdoors. Remember if a light bulb is always on, it will burn out sooner than if it is allowed to be off for periods of time. The human mind and body operate in the same manner.

Moral: I will do other things for relaxation!

Political Affiliations Mean Nothing

P

Political Affiliations Mean Nothing on the Road to Success!

Political affiliations are a way of American life. However, they mean zero toward one's success in life. There are successful Republicans in the pursuit of life and there are successful Democrats in the pursuit of life. There are also successful Americans who have no formal political affiliation. The political arena is a personal preference. One can choose to be A, B, or none of the above. That is what makes our political system great—we have individual choices. Our democratic society stands for *Life, Liberty and the Pursuit of Happiness!*

Moral: I may or may not have political affiliations—the choice is mine!

Wealth is Important

Q

Wealth Should Be a
Goal of Success!

Peace of mind is probably a main key in being successful. However, wealth is not a sin in achieving our goals. A by-product of success should be having the wealth to make independent choices and be able to pay the bills with something le.● over. One does not have to be a millionaire to be successful but should be monetarily comfortable to not only afford the necessities of life, but also to splurge on some extravagances. It is very rewarding mentally to be able to dine at a five-star restaurant occasionally and sip on a glass of fine champagne. On the way home, stop and buy the kids some gifts.

Moral: I will accumulate wealth to use!

Optimism is Vital

R

Optimism Is Positive and Vital to Success!

A person who is optimistic is always positive and sees life from the proper prospective. The optimist sees that the glass is half-full of water while the pessimist sees the glass half-empty. Successful people are optimistic. They can always turn a negative situation into positive results. Optimists are visionaries as they can see above the clouds and approach the future with an "I can do" attitude. Optimistic people are fun to be around!

Moral: I will be optimistic!

I am a Leader

S

Leaders Lead—Followers Follow!

Since the beginning of mankind there have evolved leaders and followers. Of course, there are few leaders and many followers. You must be a unique person to be a leader. You must believe in yourself, in your abilities, in your teaching capabilities. You must enjoy the leadership role and have great communication skills. Your approach must be strong, your direction concise. You must be caring about the welfare of others and you must be self-motivated. You must feel great inner satisfaction when you achieve objectives. You must relish leading others into the successes of life.

Moral: I am a leader!

Obstacles Will be Overcome

T

Obstacles Will Surface and Be Overcome on the Road to Success!

No path in life is free of obstacles. Obstacles are the challenges of life which must be faced, addressed, and conquered to succeed. If life were free of obstacles, we would all be successful and no hardships would prevail. If things are too easy, our character is not developed to its fullest. There have been many documented cases where a self-made millionaire loses their fortune only to regroup and gain it back again. The obstacles were there but the determination to succeed was greater and the obstacles were overcome.

Moral: I will overcome obstacles!

Thinking is Vital

U

Thinking Is a Vital Factor to Success!

God gave us a brain to use to control our physical attributes, but its most important function is the ability to think. That is what sets us apart from all other life forms. We can think! Through that process we can determine right from wrong. We have the ability to reason and learn. We can learn left from right, up from down, green from blue. We feel emotions such as happiness and sadness. Some use their brains more than others, developing a keen sense of the thinking process. We should all try to maximize our thought processes. Thinkers accomplish more in life.

Moral: I am a thinker!

Dress for Success

V

Dress for Success—It Counts!

People laugh about conformity, but in the business world it means a lot. The dark double-breasted suit, the white starched shirt with the red power tie, the spit-shined wing-tip shoes, the red satin handkerchief in the suit pocket, the neat close-cropped haircut, all make a statement for a professional businessman. This style of dress breeds success! For a businesswoman the double-breasted dark pin-striped suit with white silk blouse, dark pumps, dark hose, and impeccable hair design make a powerful statement. This is dress for success! If you want to be successful, you must dress the part.

Moral: I will dress for success!

Love Counts

W

Love Counts!

It is not a weakness to love someone. To the contrary, this shows a person is capable of deep feeling. Feelings are important on the road to success. One cannot always be an inanimate object or machine cranking toward a common goal. To experience love is to see the leaves from the trees, the beauty of a snowflake, what is right with the universe. Love for a spouse, for a child, or for an animal is peace of mind, and good for the heart and soul. Experience love if the opportunity presents itself.

Moral: I am capable of love!

Hard Work Counts

X

Hard Work within the Proper Framework Is Vital to Success!

To be successful at any venture in life, one must work hard. My father instilled the virtue of hard work in me at an early age. He would say, "You can attain as much in your life as you would desire, if you are willing to work hard to attain such." Working hard doesn't mean putting as many hours as you can into an endeavor. Working hard means using the resources that are available to you and staying focused with your knowledge to obtain the desired goal or result. Hard work is good for the body and mind!

Moral: I will work hard!

Obey the Law

Y

Obey the Law—Laws Protect Our Individual Rights!

The Bill of Rights was written into law by our forefathers to protect our individual rights. We have the right to the "pursuit of life, liberty, happiness, freedom of speech, right to bear arms, right to practice religion as we see fit." However, our judicial system has laws which protect individuals in our society from chaos and anarchy. We must pursue our quest for success within the framework of these laws. We can get to the top without cheating the system or breaking the laws that are here to protect us. The law is on our side.

Moral: I will obey the law!

Z

Success—Measured in Your Terms!

We have read *The ABC's of Success in Simple Terms*. We have followed these simple premises and put them into use in our daily lives. We will have a full, productive, successful life!

Moral: I am successful!

The Moral of the Story—Success!

A. I believe in myself!

B. I must understand the system!

C. I must maintain my health!

D. I will be an extrovert!

E. I believe in a higher being!

F. I will be creative!

G. I will remain focused!

H. I will win!

I. I will control stress!

J. I will document the route to the top!

K. I don't need big words to achieve!

L. I believe people are good!

M. I will have friends!

N. I need my family!

O. I will do other things for relaxation!

P. I may or may not have political affiliations—the choice is mine!

Q. I will accumulate wealth to use!

R. I will be optimistic!

S. I am a leader!

T. I will overcome obstacles!

U. I am a thinker!

V. I will dress for success!

W. I am capable of love!

X. I will work hard!

Y. I will obey the law!

Z. I am successful!

About the Author

Edward Paul Sowa is a self-made man. He grew up in modest means, and early on discovered he had leadership qualities. Large in physical stature at an early age (6'8" tall), he became an excellent athlete. He used this physical prowess to his advantage in the business world.

After years of being involved in the food industry and having much success, Edward was prodded by others to explain how he achieved his status. Edward decided to write a book about the simple principles he followed. Now that you've read the book . . . hopefully your life will have a little more meaning.